The Adventures of

BARNABAS

The Sacrificial Lamb
Leviticus

A COLORING BOOK

By Susan Sherwood Parr
Illustrated by Moira North

WORD PRODUCTIONS

Published by
Word Productions LLC ©2018

The Adventures of Barnabas: The Sacrificial Lamb Leviticus
©2018

By

Susan Sherwood Parr

Illustrations by Moira North

ISBN:

978-0-9978373-3-9

PUBLISHED BY
Word Productions LLC
www.wordproductions.org
PO BOX 11865, Albuquerque, NM 87192

Let's Take a Trip!"

Hi kids! Are you ready for an adventure? Today *we're* going to Jerusalem. *Come* on, let's *get* going!

"We're going on a trip today. No time to waste; it's time to play. We're going to have so much fun. So stop what you're doing and come on!"

1

"We're Going Back in Time"

"Kids, we're going back in time. I want you to meet a friend of mine. We've got a lot of things to do—so get on the train—we're waiting for you."

2

Just Outside Jerusalem

The lambs lived just outside the city. In the distance, Leviticus heard the sounds of people hurrying about in the marketplace as they prepared for the Passover feast.

Which Lamb Would Be Chosen?

All the lambs had been grooming themselves, and that afternoon they would parade before their master. One lamb would be selected for the Passover feast (See Ex. 12).

The Lamb for the Sacrifice

Leviticus was also busy preparing himself. Only the finest and best lamb would be picked for the Jewish Passover feast (Ex. 12:5). Their master had waited for this time all year!

Leviticus' Brother Had Been Chosen

When Leviticus' brother Lucas lived, all the lambs felt like he would *surely* be the next lamb chosen for the Great Sacrifice (Ex. 12:5-14).

A Cruel Master

All the lambs knew well that their master had been a very evil and frightening man. He seemed to enjoy killing the lambs.

Could Jesus Change Their Master?

Jesus of Nazareth had been teaching on the side of the mountain outside the city. Their master had stopped to listen. Could this make him kind? (2 Cor. 5:17).

The Parade Was Over...Leviticus Was *Not* Chosen

The lambs thought about how their master seemed different. Leviticus' mother was comforted because she still had one of her sons. They slept peacefully in the pasture that night.

9

The Next Day

What on earth is that noise mama? What are those men shouting about? Listen...

I don't know, dear. They sound angry about something.

Voices were growing louder in the distance. Because the lambs lived just outside the walls of Jerusalem, they could hear it all!

Inside the City Gate

The crowd grew louder as they begged for the release of the
wicked prisoner Barabbas. Even though Jesus Christ was an
innocent man, they wanted Him to be crucified (Matt. 27:11–26).

The Sky Became Dark

Leviticus nestled in close to his mother as the sky became dark all around the city that afternoon (Matt. 27:45).

Would A Lamb Always Have To Die?

The herd of lambs began stirring! The sky was dark and thunder rolled. The lambs were frightened.

The Temple Curtain Tears Down the Middle

The sky was dark and the thunder crashed. In the temple, the curtain was torn in half (Matt. 27:51). What was happening in the city that day? What kind of event would make the elements sway?

Jesus Hung on the Cross

The innocent Jesus had been crucified...slain, as the lambs gazed across the darkened terrain. What had happened? Why, the cross gave life through death— the Messiah's sacrifice.

Peace Filled the Darkeness

A strange but welcome quiet came over the herd of lambs. They felt peaceful.

Barnabas Has a Message...

"Kids, Jesus' sacrifice on the Cross at Calvary paid the price for our sins and the sins of the whole world."

A Messiah Would Come to Save God's People

"Long ago, a spotless lamb had to be offered in sacrifice for our sins, until the promised Messiah was sent by God (Is. 7:14; 53)."

'Jesus Was the Lamb of God"

"Jesus was the Spotless Lamb, that perfect sacrifice (John 1:29; Rev. 5:6, 12). He is the Messiah. He gave His life so that we could all live forever (John 11:25)."

Jesus Died, Saving All People...and the Lambs

"Not only did Jesus save all of mankind and the lambs' master...Jesus also saved the lives of Leviticus and the other lambs. A lamb no longer needed to be sacrificed for people's sins."

Remember These Things

Jesus is the Lamb of God (John 1:29).

Jesus died for our sins (John 3:16).

Jesus rose from the dead (Matt. 28:1–8).

Jesus is alive (Mark 16:6).

Jesus ascended into Heaven (Mark 16:19; Acts 1:9).

Jesus sits with the Father (Mark 16:19).

"Kids, if you would like to ask Jesus into your heart today, pray this prayer right now:"

Dearest Lord Jesus,
I believe that You died for my sins
and the sins of the whole world.
Please forgive me of all of my sins
and come into my heart right now.
I believe that You died on the cross for me
and that You have risen from the dead.
I make You the Lord and Savior of my life.
Take control of my life and make me into
the kind of person You want me to be.

Amen

(John 3:16; Rom. 10:9–10)

My Own Comic Book

www.ingramcontent.com/pod-product-compliance
Lightning Source LLC
Chambersburg PA
CBHW081237020426
42331CB00012B/3212